SHADOW MAGIC

SHADOW MAGIC

CREATE 75 CREATURES

Sophie Collins

IVY PRESS

This edition published in the UK and North America in 2020 by
Ivy Press
An imprint of The Quarto Group
The Old Brewery, 6 Blundell Street
London N7 9BH, United Kingdom
T (0)20 7700 6700
www.QuartoKnows.com

The projects in this book were first published in
Shadow Art/The Art of Making Shadows (2007).

British Library Cataloguing-in-Publication Data
A catalogue record for this book is available from the British Library

ISBN: 978-0-7112-5739-9

This book was conceived, designed, and produced by
Ivy Press
Creative Director **Peter Bridgewater**
Publisher **Jason Hook**
Editorial Director **Caroline Earle**
Senior Project Editor **Dominique Page**
Art Director **Sarah Howerd**
Project Designer **Joanna Clinch**
Page Make-up **Lyndsey Harwood**
Illustrator **John Woodcock**

Printed in China

Contents

6 Introduction to Shadow Art

8 How to Show Your Shadows

10 Hand and Finger Exercises

12 Practicing Basic Shapes

14 **The Animals**

16 Single-hand Animals

36 Two-hand Animals

94 Challenging Animals

148 Advanced Animals

174 Index

176 Resources

Introduction to Shadow Art

Making shadow animals is a great pastime. With just a small amount of flexibility, a flashlight (or a couple of light sources, if you want to get more elaborate), and at least one pair of hands, you can create a farmyard full of animals. First made popular a century and a half ago, before radio, television, the internt, or video games, hand shadows appeared in many manuals of polite entertainment. One children's encyclopedia published in 1901 claims that "any clever boy or girl" should be able to put on a shadow show of half an hour or so for their friends and relations, and makes suggestions for several playlets, from *Punch and Judy* to the *Babes in the Wood*.

Making shadows a hundred years ago: the surroundings look solemn and the shadow-caster is formally clad—but the wolf on the screen is just the same as the one you will find in this menagerie.

Of course you might not want to go so far, but even in its simplest form there's something compulsive about shadow-casting—first, using just a flashlight, you might try an easy horse or dog shape, then, encouraged by the surprisingly lifelike results, progress to a leaping squirrel or a hopping rabbit. You'll find that you become competitive with family and friends— "That's your pig? Wait till you see my turkey!", and soon you'll be making the sounds that go along with the animals. Shadow art is a great diversion for little kids around bedtime, and a way of luring older ones away from their constant console-tapping; they just won't be able to resist demonstrating how they can get a better result than you.

This book contains all you need to become an impressive shadow artist. First comes advice and guidance on how to create and show your shadows. Then you will find seventy-five animal shapes, graded by difficulty. When you've got through all the single-hand ones, move on to the two-hand shadows— and, when you have all those mastered, flex your fingers, flap your wrists, and have a shot at the rhinoceros, the peacock, or the mole. This is inclusive entertainment—even the smallest fingers, at one end of the family, or the most arthritic ones, at the other, can master the basic swallow, or make a snapping crocodile, and most people will enjoy the challenge of the hardest animals, right at the end of the book.

How to Show
Your Shadows

The most basic form of shadow-casting calls for just a darkened room, a flashlight or other light source (although it must be local, and not too diffuse — an angled worklamp is ideal), and a pale wall or other surface, such as a blind, on which to cast your shadows. Most shadow-casters will also want an audience — although there's some personal satisfaction in getting the perfect outline and movement of an elephant's trunk or a gobbling turkey, it will be all the greater if there's someone else there with you to gasp at your achievement, or with whom you can take turns.

Starter method

Start off with a worklamp or a flashlight propped securely with books or on a cushion. It can be placed at any height that it will be comfortable to move your hands in front of. It should cast a clear circle of light onto the wall — around two feet in diameter. This will give you enough space to make the animal shape with a clear margin around it. The shadow cast should be clear-edged and dark. Experiment by holding your hand between the light source and the wall until you find the distance at which your shadow animals will show clearly. You will get the most impressive results by forming your animal first, out of the light, and then moving it, fully formed, into the light.

Performance method

When you've reached the point at which your repertoire is worth boasting about, you can try a slightly more elaborate setup. Your rapt audience sits on a high-backed couch facing the "screen." You kneel behind the couch, with as many accomplices as you need, ready to hold up your hands in animal form behind the couch back (the line of the back is the base of your "stage"). Your primary light source (a lamp or a flashlight) illuminates your hands from behind, so that their shadows are cast on to the wall. If you want two layers of shadow, then you could create scenery by cutting out background shapes from pieces of card. You can place your background on a table or other flat surface and put a second light source (a table lamp, for example) behind it, as shown in the diagram. Your animals will appear in darker shadow, with the paler outline of the prop scene behind them.

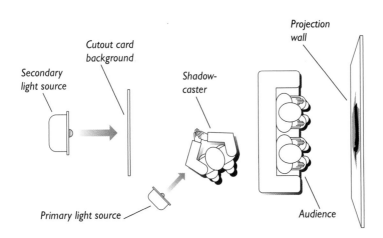

Secondary light source

Cutout card background

Shadow-caster

Projection wall

Primary light source

Audience

Hand and Finger Exercises

While anyone can make the easiest shadow animals, if you want to manage the whole menagerie you'll need to exercise your hands and fingers. Keen video game enthusiasts may find that they have an advantage here, and that their fingers are already very flexible. If your hands are stiff, however, run them through a quick calisthenics class before you start making shapes. A couple of minutes spent stretching and flexing will make even stiff hands much more agile. You will find that you have a leading hand, and may find it easier to use this to make the harder parts of the animals—remember, you can always reverse the animal positions and the directions in which they move if you find it easier to create a shape the other way around.

1 Start by clenching both hands and then extending the fingers and stretching each finger, one by one, to its fullest extent.

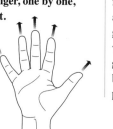

2 Hold your little and your ring finger, and your middle and forefinger together in two pairs, and create a "V"-shaped gap between them, without allowing gaps to appear between the paired fingers.

3 Curl each finger of your right hand into the palm, one by one, while keeping the other fingers stretched straight out. Most people find this easy with their forefinger, but progressively harder moving down the fingers and very hard when they come to the little finger. Repeat until you find it quite easy to do, then run through the same exercise with your left hand.

4 Starting from the little finger and ring finger of your right hand, curl your fingers down to the palm in pairs, while keeping the other fingers stretched straight out (little and ring fingers, ring and middle fingers, middle and forefinger). When you can do this easily, repeat the exercise with your left hand.

5 Repeat exercise 4, but instead of curling the paired fingers down to the palm, bring them to meet your thumb, while keeping the other fingers stretched straight out. Work through this with your right hand first, then your left.

6 To finish, let both hands hang limply down and circle them half a dozen times, flexing your wrists.

Practicing Basic Shapes

On these pages, we've reproduced three of the simplest animals to make—the German Shepherd dog, the crocodile, and the elephant, with annotation, showing you the order in which to form the shapes, and bend your fingers. Bear in mind that the shapes of people's hands can vary quite dramatically, and that this can make small differences to the final shadows. It may also affect which shapes you find hardest to make—if you have square palms and short fingers, rounded shapes such as the bear cub will be easier for you to do than more attenuated ones like the kangaroo. Keep practicing, and you'll soon identify your favorite shadow animals: those that are easiest for you to make, and most impressive to show.

As you work your way through the menagerie, you'll inevitably find some shadows easier to make than others. Broadly, we've arranged them in the order in which you might try them—from the simplest to the hardest to make. This isn't rigid, though—you might find some that we've cited as "hard" easier to make than you expected. It all depends on the individual shape and flexibility of your hands.

Brace both thumbs upward

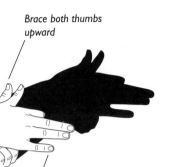

Hold a steady gap between the little finger and the rest of the hand

Keep the back of your hand in an even curve

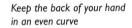

Brace your little finger and forefinger upward, while keeping the trunk pointing steadily down

Hold the bent angle of the fingers as you open and shut your hands

The Animals

Organized in four sections, in order of difficulty, our menagerie consists of seventy-five animals, ranging from the humble jellyfish to the haughty camel and the growling grizzly.

Single-Hand Animals

These animals are easiest to make because you only have to worry about the shape and positioning of one hand. Pay close attention to the angle of your hand and arm in relation to the light source, to ensure that your shadow appears straight and clear on the wall.

Swallow

Surely the simplest shadow to make of all. "Swoop" your hand forward in big arcs, moving your paired fingers as you do so to represent the swallow's wings. Keep the thumb braced out as your bird flies, so that the swallow's neck remains outstretched as he darts around.

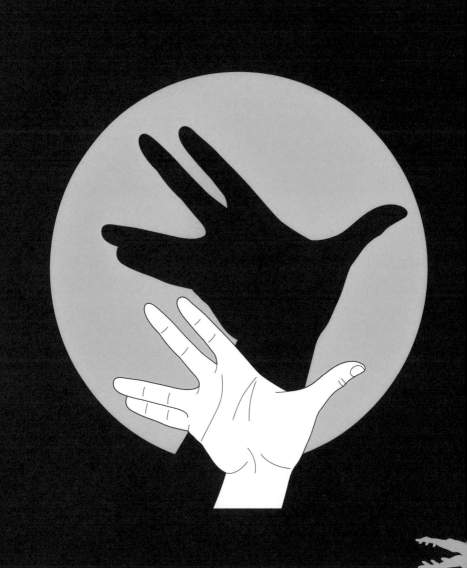

Goose

This is one of the simplest shadows, and a great starter position. The only possible difficulty you may have is in moving your little finger up and down (to open and shut the beak) without simultaneously moving it in and out. Try thrusting your hand forward and down, then pulling it sharply back, to give the impression of the goose's waddle.

Salamander

The salamander's long, lizardlike head and the draped skin beneath his jaw can be made easily with your left hand. Tuck in your little finger and your thumb as much as is needed to get the silhouette to look just right: this is such a simple shape that it needs to be made quite carefully to give a good impression.

Baby Giraffe

The shadow of the giraffe's calf is formed more simply than the parent's outline (*see pages 60–61*). You can make the giraffe roam around and turn her head by flexing your wrist slightly while "walking" her forward.

Starling

Starlings constantly chatter and shriek, so you can rapidly open and shut the beak of this shadow to make it talk. Pull your little and your ring fingers in, then bend them a bit, and you will find that you are able to make shorter-beaked species, such as sparrows or thrushes. In many nineteenth-century manuals of what was then called "shadowgraphy," this easy-to-form silhouette served as an all-purpose, all-species bird shadow.

Duck

The duck is easy to make. Scissor your fingers for a quacking duck, while making the appropriate sound effect. Raising the head sharply, as shown, while quacking loudly, allows the duck to sound the alarm—perhaps as one of the predator species moves too close for comfort.

Greyhound

If you have short-fingered hands you will be able to form the most recognizable greyhound head. If you have longer fingers, therefore creating a face that looks too elongated, angle your hand slightly toward the wall: this will shorten the dog's nose a little. If you can, also angle your thumb toward the wall a fraction, to make a suitably narrow ear for a sighthound.

Snake

This is a very straightforward silhouette to form: the snake's flickering tongue is made from two blades of grass or tiny slips of paper tucked between the middle and forefinger of the left hand. You can move your whole arm sharply forward to make the snake "strike."

Monkey

You use only your left hand to make the monkey, but it is difficult to fold your knuckles and fingers tidily to make the hunched shape of his head and shoulder convincing, and you may need to practice for a while to get the right silhouette. Use the heel of your hand and the curve of your forearm to make the monkey's lower body.

Two-Hand Animals

The animals in this section use both hands, but are relatively simple to make. You will find that some of them look most lifelike if you hold them still; others, however, will spring into life if you move your conjoined hands in a suitable way—snapping for the crocodile, say, and lowering and extending the neck for the swan.

Shark

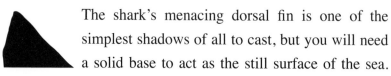

The shark's menacing dorsal fin is one of the simplest shadows of all to cast, but you will need a solid base to act as the still surface of the sea. You can teach the smallest child this shadow, so it's a useful addition to the repertoire for a family or group shadow session. Tilt the conjoined hands backward a little as you move the shark forward through the water. Even if you can resist humming the theme tune for the movie *Jaws* as you do so, your audience is unlikely to show such restraint.

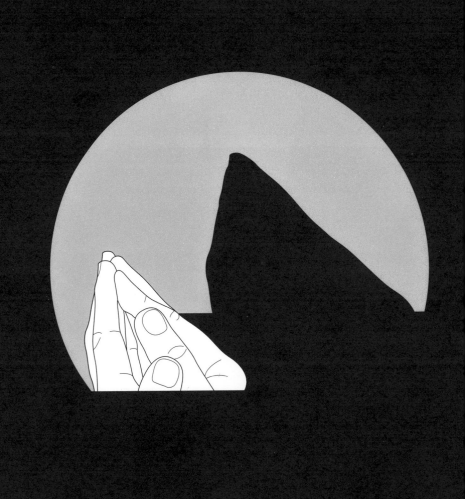

Jellyfish

 The jellyfish is quite simple to make, and, if you wobble all the downward-facing fingers slightly as you move it forward, is also a very convincing swimmer.

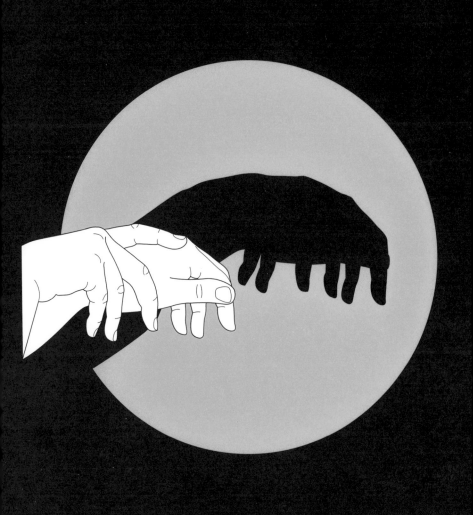

Dove

This is one of the simplest shapes of all. Overlap your thumbs a little to give the bird both a head and a beak. The dove is usually seen in flight, an effect that is achieved by flapping both your hands to and fro, but it must fly in a straight line—if it soars, the illusion will be spoiled by too much of your forearms becoming visible.

German Shepherd

As its name suggests, the German Shepherd dog is a herding breed. This shadow is extremely easy to do: if you keep the mouth open, your dog will have a fierce, intent look; close it for a gentler, more reflective profile.

Billy Goat

The billy goat has prominent horns, a long profile, and, like the nanny goat (*see pages 140–141*), a small, neat beard. This is a simpler shadow to make than that of the nanny goat, and it has an unsophisticated look. Nonetheless, as part of a farmyard scene it can work surprisingly well.

Horse

This simple outline can look surprisingly equine, provided you get the angle between your thumbs and palms right for the horse's head. Practice moving the little finger of your right hand up and down, so that your shadow horse can open and shut its mouth, while keeping the lower two fingers of your left hand tucked away behind your right palm, in order to keep the silhouette clear and clean.

Crab

The crab is a very easy shadow to form. As soon as you have a realistic outline, make your crab move by shuffling it rapidly sideways, moving all its legs at once, and hiding your forearms behind the stage edge.

Swan

The swan is one of the most elegant shadow silhouettes, and you can "sail" it along the back of your stage edge in a very stately manner. The right hand, forming the wing, should disappear behind your left upper arm at the wrist, so that your swan shadow doesn't have any breaks in its overall outline.

Crocodile

Snippety-snap! The crocodile can be made to snap his jaws simply by opening and closing your hands sharply. Move your hands across your stage from left to right as you do so, making a snapping noise.

Snail

The simple snail is easily made. Because the shape involves both your forearms as well as your hands, you will need to move your whole body in order for it to slither across the picture. Practice sliding over whichever high surface forms your "stage" edge, while still holding the snail shadow. Wave the eye-stalks a little as your snail moves.

Bear Cub

In contrast to the fierce-looking adult bear (*see pages 98–99*), the bear cub has a soft, blunt face, with its ears pricked up in curiosity. The top of the head is easily made with a clenched left hand, while the bear cub's muzzle is formed by the flattened fingers of your right hand, carefully angled into position. Try slowly turning your left hand to make your bear cub's ears move.

Giraffe

Your right hand should be held in as clean a line as possible so that the giraffe's neck looks smooth and doesn't have any bumps. Raise the knuckle of the forefinger of your left hand to give the giraffe his eye bump. Practice wiggling the fingers of your left hand very slightly so that the head can dip forward and the nose can twitch a little as the giraffe's neck sways forward.

Jackal

The jackal has a rather doglike head, but also a mane of fur that runs along the center line of his back, giving the appearance of permanently raised hackles. The mane is created with the knuckles of your right hand, ranged down the neck (your left wrist) of your shadow shape.

Rat

Although your right hand supports your left and helps you to broaden the rat's neck, this is essentially a one-hand shadow, and is not particularly difficult to make. Slips of paper or blades of grass act as effective whiskers and will twitch realistically as you move your middle and ring fingers slightly to and fro so that the rat wiggles his nose.

Red Deer

The red deer is distinguished by his imposing antlers, which are easy to form with the fingers of your right hand. If you practice with a friend, you can make your shadow stags fight realistically by lowering their heads and horns, then moving them sharply toward one another, and letting their antlers "clash."

Roe Deer

The roe deer's strongest characteristics are its long, oval eye, and its horns, which are angled well forward in front of its ear. This is one of those shadows that is easy to approximate but quite hard to get perfect. Practice in order to balance the shape correctly. Like the red deer species (*see pages 66–67*), when you've made a lifelike roe deer, you can make her graze by plucking up small, previously gathered tufts of grass.

Turkey

The turkey is harder to make than it looks. Your left hand should be kept well tucked under your right, with the thumb held in under the palm. When you have a shadow that looks like a turkey, try wobbling the lowered fingers of your left hand so that the turkey's wattles shake as it moves forward. Make a gobbling sound for added realism.

Bull

The finger shape for the bull is similar to that of the cow (*see pages 74–75*), but the bull has a blunter face and more strongly curved horns. If you'd like your bull to wear a ring through his nose all you need to do is twist a paperclip into a neat circle and fix it at a slight angle—so that it reflects as a ring, and not simply as a line—between the middle and forefinger of your right hand.

Cow

This is a simple silhouette, but you may find it quite hard at first to curl your left thumb round flexibly to make the cow's second horn. Practice bending and rotating both thumbs in as full a circle as you can.

Water Buffalo

The water buffalo is formed in a manner similar to that of the bull (*see pages 72–73*) but his wider, curving horns are made by curling the thumb and forefinger of your left hand strongly outward. This is one shadow in which longer fingers will have the advantage—you will be able to get a more impressive spread and breadth for the buffalo's horns. As with the bull shadow, you can make a ring to lead the buffalo with a paperclip bent into a ring, or a readymade curtain ring, inserted between the middle and forefinger of your right hand. You can even tie a string to it, so that your buffalo can be led.

Fox

The fox is not a particularly difficult shadow to make, but the fingers of your left hand should be overlapped as much as necessary to make his face as pointed as possible, or you will find that the resulting creature looks more horselike than vulpine. You should keep your thumbs angled, too, until the fox's ears are realistically pointed.

Butterfly

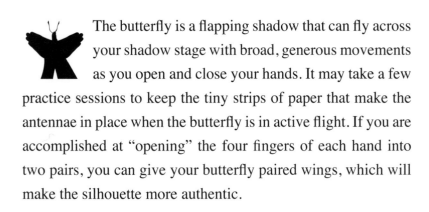 The butterfly is a flapping shadow that can fly across your shadow stage with broad, generous movements as you open and close your hands. It may take a few practice sessions to keep the tiny strips of paper that make the antennae in place when the butterfly is in active flight. If you are accomplished at "opening" the four fingers of each hand into two pairs, you can give your butterfly paired wings, which will make the silhouette more authentic.

Raven

The raven's silhouette is much more hunched and less open than that of the dove (*see pages 42–43*); it is portrayed while huddled on a branch, rather than in full flight. The head and upper body are formed with a curled right hand, while the left hand is held open and flat, so that the raven can stretch out one of its wings.

Toad

As you might expect, the toad is formed in a similar way to the frog (*see pages 90–91*), but with a more pronounced eye hump and a deeper, smoother throat (for a lower, bass croak). Round out the back of your right hand down to the wrist to swell the throat, and then bring it in again, making a croaking noise as the toad "exhales."

Hippopotamus

If you have long, slender hands, you may need to fold in the fingers of your left hand rather than keep the palm and fingers flat, as shown, to give your hippopotamus a convincingly blunt lower jaw. Although this is a comparatively simple shape to form, it demands that your left hand be flexible and may take more practice than you expect. Open and shut the hippopotamus's jaws and roar loudly to complete the fearsome impression.

Moose

The moose is very similar to that of the red deer (*see pages 66–67*), but the upper hand is curved more, so that the palm of your left hand gives the impression of the broader areas of a moose's antlers. The moose's complex upper mouth and jaw are formed by keeping the fingers of your right hand overlapping rather than even at the ends.

Frog

The frog's throat needs to be held in a smooth curve, with a soft angle where your right hand meets your wrist. Use your top (left) hand to open and shut the mouth, relaxing your lower hand a little to create a swell in the frog's neck. Make a throaty croaking noise as you move the mouth, and "hop" your frog across the frame by jumping both hands simultaneously, holding the shape in place as you do so.

Alpaca

Alpacas have a ball of wool, which looks somewhat like a pompon, growing on top of their head between their ears, giving them a very different profile from that of the llama (*see pages 108–109*). This shadow clearly shows the bulk between the ears of the alpaca, as well as the slightly hunched back, although not humped dramatically like that of a camel—just a little rounded.

Challenging Animals

The intermediate members of the menagerie, some of these shadows will take a little practice to make effectively. Be patient and work your way through them—when you can form all the animals in this section, you're well on your way to becoming a shadow virtuoso.

Rabbit

The rabbit's long ears and whiffling nose are his most characteristic features, and you can easily give the impression of both with this shadow. Bend the two upright fingers of your right hand at the knuckle, then jerk them upright again to make the rabbit sense a distraction, while moving the three lowered fingers of your left hand to and fro very slightly to make your rabbit's nose twitch with anticipation. Keep the ear movements abrupt and the nose movements subtle to create the most realistic-looking shadow rabbit.

Bear

The growling bear's shadow shows ears, gaping jaws, and front and back legs, so you need to place your individual fingers carefully to make a balanced shape. Tuck your right thumb neatly behind your left hand, and form the head and ears first. When you have the pointed ears and the face shape, use the thumb of your left hand to make the lower leg, and the little and ring fingers to make the foreleg. This is a shadow that doesn't move—if you want it to walk, make the head only, and move the shadow down so that the lower parts of your hands are concealed behind the surface (couch back or equivalent) that you are using as your stage "floor."

Pig

The hardest aspect of making the pig is extending the little and ring fingers of your right hand just the correct amount to give the impression of the pig's little legs and trotters. Also, the throat needs to have a smooth curve up to the snout for your hand shadow to look sufficiently porcine. A little practice will ensure that you achieve a properly piglike outline. Snort and snuffle through your nose, and move your "leg" fingers lightly to and fro to make the pig trot forward.

Elephant

Keep the crevice in the right hand tiny — it forms the elephant's small but characterful eye. The trunk can be upraised (with accompanying trumpeting sound) by turning your left hand the other way up and curling your ring finger upward, but you can't do this as the elephant is progressing magisterially — you will have to withdraw your hands and then re-form the head. Practice doing this quickly so that the gap in your performance isn't noticeable.

Crow

A short, blunt tail and a strong outline make the crow instantly recognizable. He makes a good shadow to include in a woodland scene, perhaps observing while the dove and the swallow (*see pages 42–43 and 18–19*), which are both easier shadows to move, fly to and fro. You can duck the crow's head forward onto his breast and down to his side if you like, to create the impression that he is grooming his feathers.

Vulture

This scavenging bird looks like no other, and the hunched shoulders and powerful beak make its shadow rendition instantly recognizable. Getting your fingers into position is straightforward, but keeping the beak in place while forming your fingers into the "hump" of the back is harder; it's easiest to make the bird in two parts—positioning each hand separately—and then putting them together.

Llama

The llama's face is raised and its ears are alert. This creature is formed in a similar way to the head of the peacock (*see pages 112–113*), but with a wider, smoother chest (and, of course, no tail!). Crook the middle and little fingers of your right hand to move the llama's face.

Possum

The possum has long ears, a sharp, pointed profile, and strong jaws. The challenge of this particular shadow lies not in the positioning of your hands but in the angle of their position between the light source and your screen. If you find the shadow doesn't look like the one in the picture, swivel your conjoined hands slightly round to the right and you should find that your shadow falls into shape.

Peacock

 The peacock is a magnificent bird. The position of the right hand is straightforward to obtain—tilt it up and then down to make the peacock display his tail. The left hand must be held in a smooth line to create the peacock's outthrust breast, angled beak, and feathered topknot.

Bulldog

The bulldog has a rounded, blunt face and a keen, triangular eye. The most difficult aspect of forming this shadow is keeping the join between the upper part of the face and the muzzle smooth; tuck the fingertips of your left hand in between the knuckles of your right to make the shadow look convincing and all-of-a-piece.

Wild Boar

The wild boar's fierce profile is quite different from the gentle curves of the domestic pig. The tusk is made by flexing the forefinger of your left hand strongly upward. A small, slightly mean-looking eye adds to the overall predatory appearance, and you can make the long snout twitch by moving the middle, ring, and little fingers of the left hand, being careful to keep them together as you do so.

Cougar

 Unlike the shadows of the other big cats, the cougar is shown with a closed mouth. His blunt face is not difficult to form, but he is hard to move convincingly. If your cougar is intently watching the shadow of some potential prey—a rabbit, for instance—then you can establish his fierce concentration by pushing the thumb of your left hand forward with tiny movements to convey the twitching of his ears.

Owl

Large, round eyes make this simple shadow instantly recognizable as that of an owl—and you can open and close the owl's eyes with slight movements of the thumbs and forefingers of both your hands. Practice until you can move them simultaneously, or open and close just one to make your owl blink. The owl's small upright ears are positioned at the corners of his head, and are formed by gently angling your little fingers inward.

Anteater

The anteater has a very characteristic movement of the head—he walks forward with his long nose extended, then pauses and does a sweep from side to side looking for his next meal of ants or other insects. As you move his head, straighten out his nose a little, keeping your hands carefully together, then move them slowly from left to right before resuming your anteater's forward motion.

King Cobra

The king cobra is formed in a way very similar to that of the ordinary snake (*see pages 32–33*), but your right hand is called into play to give the ruler of the snake world a fittingly impressive hood. It can be tricky to get the grip across your left wrist fashioned to make the hood broad enough, so practice until your cobra looks realistic whether he is simply standing and swaying, hood outstretched, or leaning forward ready to strike.

Mole

To make a convincing mole shadow is more difficult than it looks. The overall outline is made in a similar way to that of the pig (*see pages 100–101*), but with a shallower, smoother head, a longer, less defined snout, and short flipperlike paws. The two fingers forming the snout can be moved slightly to make the mole's nose "twitch" as it is raised above the earth. Rather than moving from left to right, your mole shadow should emerge from the stage vertically, just like a real mole digging itself out of the soil.

Hare

It's easy to wiggle the hare's expressive ears, but making the shadow jump is more difficult. Practice pulling the thumb of your left hand sharply down, then "leaping" your joined hands upward while returning your thumb to a horizontal position. Managing this while keeping the forelegs in place and without either enlarging or losing the tiny gap in your fingers which makes the eye poses quite a challenge, and one that you may need a little time to get right.

Sheep

The sheep is harder to make than it looks—the nose needs to be quite blunt and the mouth open just the right amount to give a properly sheeplike impression. Tuck the middle finger of your right hand down at a sharp angle to make the eye the correct shape. When you've mastered the outline, make your sheep graze and baa by lowering and raising the head and opening and closing the mouth.

Antelope

The antelope has an extended snout and tall horns. Keep the thumb of your right hand and the little finger of your left tucked well in and down, out of sight, to ensure you achieve a good, clean shadow outline. Tilt both hands forward and down to make the antelope "graze"— you can even let him pull up a tuft of previously picked grass, tucked neatly between the ring and little fingers of your right hand for added verisimilitude.

Kangaroo

 The kangaroo shadow doesn't require any particular flexibility in your fingers, and the hand positions are not at all complex, but you will certainly need to experiment to get the relative angles of the head, tail, and legs just right. The longer your fingers, the easier you will find this shadow to make—but, given time, it is possible for even the short-fingered to achieve a convincing result!

Tortoise

 This is a simple shape to form, but another one that it is hard to move realistically. The tortoise can be made to walk forward in the authentic, lumbering manner by moving each leg forward, one at a time. This is a good shadow to use to practice movement, as even relatively stiff fingers can eventually be formed into a realistic motion.

Donkey

The challenge of this shadow is to make a neat little gap between the ring and little fingers of your right hand for the donkey's eye, while keeping all the fingers of your left hand neatly tucked in to give it a solid, convincing nose. When you've mastered the shape, see if you can fling his head back and open his mouth (separating the little and ring fingers of your left hand) to make the donkey bray.

Nanny Goat

Keep the curve of the nanny goat's profile smooth, with only a slight angle where your right hand makes contact with your left. The nanny goat's horns point well forward, with a small, raised ear formed by your thumb behind them. The beard is an especially expressive feature, and you can make it wag by flexing your little finger to and fro.

Woodpecker

As you would expect, the woodpecker has a powerful beak. The long, forked tail descends below the branch on which it sits. If you have a stable upright that you can use as a tree trunk, you can imitate the action of the bird by rapidly advancing and withdrawing the beak against the trunk, making the characteristic "hammering" peck. Keep your left hand still and use your right to show the woodpecker at work.

Cat

The proportions of the cat are relatively hard to get right, although its head is easily learned. If your left hand is flexible you will find that you can curl its back into a catlike curve before extending your forefinger for its tail. For a longer body, extend your left hand further beyond your right, but keep the angle between head and body in a curve—if it becomes sharp, the cat shape will be lost.

Cockerel

The bottom half of the cockerel's head is formed like that of the turkey (*see pages 70–71*), but the crest is made by tilting three fingers of the left hand upward, instead of folding them across the top of the head. You need flexible fingers and plenty of practice to get all the angles right and to make the cockerel appear lifelike.

Advanced Animals

This group of animals demands great flexibility in your fingers, hands, and wrists, and the ability not only to make but also to hold an awkward position in order to achieve a satisfactory shadow. Be prepared to practice—the results will be worth it.

Wolf

The wolf has a narrow, intense eye and open, menacing jaws. Practice keeping the pupil in place as you move the wolf forward. In time, you can learn to open and shut the toothy jaws, although at first you will find it hard to keep your paired fingers crossed as you do so.

Coyote

The coyote's jaw is formed in the same way as that of the wolf (*see pages 150–151*), but it has a bonier, more elongated head, formed by the ridges of the knuckles of your right hand. Its ears are long, and angled forward. You can make it howl by tilting the whole head upward and vibrating (rather than closing) the jaws. At first you will find it hard to move the head while keeping your paired fingers crossed, but eventually you will be able to do so quite easily.

Mouse

Getting all of your fingers into the correct alignment to make the mouse is hard, but this shadow is worth practicing, as it is one of the most lifelike of all in movement—just wriggle the extended finger of your left hand to wave the tail while crooking the little finger of your right to "walk" the front leg forward. If you are finding the shadow very difficult, try making the mouse at first without the eye—this will allow you to hold your hand more loosely. Do take the trouble to add tiny straw or paper whiskers, though, as they will add greatly to the impression of "mouse."

Rhinoceros

A long blunt nose with a central tusk or horn characterizes the rhinoceros, and this is made by extending the little finger of the right hand beyond the slightly curled fingers of the left. The trick is to angle your little finger against the light in such a way as to thicken the appearance of the horn; if you point it away from the light and toward the wall just a bit you will find that the resulting horn is satisfactorily hefty to match the animal's fearsome reputation.

Tiger

To create the tiger you will need a cloth or towel that you can drape right around both wrists to form the ear and the neck, as shown. Practice by first getting the drape of the fabric in place, then moving your hands gently into position to form the tiger's authentically toothy profile.

Lion

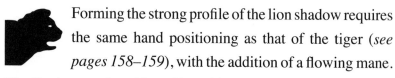 Forming the strong profile of the lion shadow requires the same hand positioning as that of the tiger (*see pages 158–159*), with the addition of a flowing mane. The lion's mane is achieved by taking a length of fabric (towel, T-shirt, or rumpled cotton shirt—anything will serve provided that it is light enough to be draped to give it some volume) and wrapping it around your wrists and the top of your left hand, rumpling it to give it the appearance of waves. You will need a helper to arrange the cloth after you have placed your hands.

Jaguar

The jaguar is formed in a similar way to the panther (*see pages 172–173*), but has a blunter nose, which looks slightly wrinkled. You could make a low snarl to match its appearance, poised to strike on some unwary prey. The fingers of your right hand must be neatly aligned to give the muzzle a realistic line, and you should keep the ear small and swiveled forward to match the animal's concentration.

Squirrel

When you have mastered this realistic squirrel it can be made to leap along an angled branch if you have one you can use as a prop. Create the lifelike small "jumping" movements with the little finger and thumb of your left hand as you curl and uncurl the little finger of your right hand. You need a very flexible right hand and wrist to get the shape just right; if you have difficulty, try flexing and circling your wrists a few times and then try again.

Sea Anemone

The sea anemone need only gently move its arms once it is formed, but it requires extremely flexible fingers to make—try bending your fingers to and fro in twos before attempting to make the four conjoined pairs of arms that give the anemone its characteristic outline.

Camel

The camel's most characteristic facial feature is a "whiffle" of its double top lip. You can emulate this by wiggling the forefinger of your left hand very slightly when the you have formed the camel's head. Move your conjoined hands jerkily up and down as you walk the camel forward to mimic his swaying gait.

Terrier

The terrier is one of the few shadow animals that is shown complete, with a long back and an eager, upright tail. None of the upright shadows are overly difficult to form in themselves, but obtaining a perfect shadow with mouth, eye, and legs all clearly aligned and in place will certainly take some practice, and moving your terrier is challenging—if you tilt your hands forward a little it can move forward jerkily, but the movement will never be very natural!

Panther

Predators are easiest to show with aggressively open mouths, waiting to pounce on unsuspecting prey. If you curl the fingers of your right hand in and down slightly you can make your panther snarl (keep any sound effects very low for the best effect—most predators snarl and growl in a quiet, steady note).

Index

A

alpaca 92–93
animals, advanced
 148–173
animals, challenging
 94–147
animals, for single hands,
 16–35
animals, for two hands,
 36–93
anteater 122–123
antelope 132–133

B

bear 98–99
bear cub 58–59
billy goat 46–47
boar, wild 116–117
bull 72–73
bulldog 114–115
butterfly 80–81

C

camel 168–169
cat 144–145
cobra, king 124–125
cockerel 146–147
cougar 118–119
cow 74–75
coyote 152–153
crab 50–51
crocodile 54–55
crow 104–105

D

deer, moose 88–89
deer, red 66–67
deer, roe 68–69
dog, bulldog 114–115
dog, German Shepherd
 44–45
dog, terrier 170–171
donkey 138–139

dove 42–43
duck 28–29

E

elephant 102–103

F

finger exercises 10–11
fox 78–79
frog 90–91

G

German Shepherd dog
 44–45
giraffe, adult 60–61
giraffe, baby 24–25
goat 46–47, 140–141
goose 20–21
greyhound 30–31

H
hand and finger exercises
  10–11
hare 128–129
hippopotamus 86–87
horse 48–49

J
jackal 62–63
jaguar 162–163
jellyfish 40–41

K
kangaroo 134–135
king cobra 124–125

L
lion 160–161
llama 108–109

M
mole 126–127
monkey 34–35
moose 88–89
mouse 154–155

N
nanny goat 140–141

O
owl 120–121

P
panther 172–173
peacock 112–113
pig 100–101
possum 110–111

R
rabbit 96–97
rat 64–65
raven 82–83
red deer 66–67
rhinoceros 156–157
roe deer 68–69

S
salamander 22–23
sea anemone 166–167
shark 38–39
sheep 130–131
showing your shadows
  8–9
snail 56–57
snake 32–33
snake, king cobra
  124–125
squirrel 164–165
starling 26–27

swallow 18–19
swan 52–53

T
terrier 170–171
tiger 158–159
toad 84–85
tortoise 136–137
turkey 70–71

V
vulture 106–107

W
water buffalo 76–77
wild boar 116–117
wolf 150–151
woodpecker 142–143

Resources

The range of books on shadow art generally is not wide, but the following include non-animal shadows—profiles of famous people, or shadows of human "characters," which you can use to broaden your repertoire:

The Art of Hand Shadows, Albert Almoznino, Dover, 1970

Hand Shadows, Tobar, 1997 (a reprint of *Shadowgraphs Anyone Can Make*, first published in 1927)

Fun With Hand Shadows, Sati Achath, Contemporary Books, 1996